LIVING A LIFE
OF WORSHIP

JESUS CALLING BIBLE STUDY SERIES

LIVING A LIFE OF WORSHIP

EIGHT SESSIONS

Sarah Young

with Karen Lee-Thorp

THOMAS NELSON
Since 1798

NASHVILLE   MEXICO CITY   RIO DE JANEIRO

Published in Nashville, Tennessee, by Nelson Books, an imprint of Thomas Nelson. Nelson Books and Thomas Nelson are registered trademarks of HarperCollins Christian Publishing, Inc.

All Scripture quotations, unless otherwise indicated, are taken from The Holy Bible, *New International Version*®, NIV®. Copyright © 1973, 1978, 1984, 2011 by Biblica, Inc.® Used by permission. All rights reserved worldwide.

Scripture quotations marked ESV are taken from *The Holy Bible, English Standard Version,* copyright © 2001 by Crossway Bibles, a division of Good News Publishers. Used by permission. All rights reserved.

Scripture quotations marked NKJV are taken from the New King James Version. Copyright © 1982 by Thomas Nelson, Inc. Used by permission. All rights reserved.

ISBN 978-0-7180-3588-4

First Printing May 2015 / Printed in the United States of America

CONTENTS

INTRODUCTION

Sometimes our busy and difficult lives give us the impression that God is silent. We cry out to Him, but our feelings tell us that He isn't answering our prayers. In this, our feelings are incorrect. God hears our prayers and speaks right into the situations in which we find ourselves. The trouble is that our lives are often too hectic, our minds too distracted, for us to take in what God offers.

This *Jesus Calling* Bible study is designed to help individuals and groups meditate on the words of Scripture and hear them not just as words said to people long ago but as words said to us today in the here and now. The goal is to help the heart hear and respond to what the mind reads—to encounter the living God as He speaks through the Scriptures. The writer to the Hebrews tells us:

In the past God spoke to our ancestors through the prophets at many times and in various ways, but in these last days he has spoken to us by his Son, whom he appointed heir of all things, and through whom also he made the universe. The Son is the radiance of God's glory and the exact representation of his being, sustaining all things by his powerful word.

—HEBREWS 1:1–3

God has spoken to us through His Son, Jesus Christ. The New Testament gives us the chance to walk with Jesus, see what He does, and hear Him speak into the sometimes confusing situations in which we find ourselves. The Old Testament tells us the story of how God prepared a people to be the family of Jesus, and in the experiences of those men and women we find our own lives mirrored.

THE GOAL OF THIS SERIES

The *Jesus Calling Bible Study Series* offers you a chance to lay down your cares, enter God's Presence, and hear Him speak through His Word. You will get to spend some time in silence studying a passage of Scripture, and if you're meeting with a group, you'll get to share your insights and hear what others discovered. You'll also get to discuss excerpts from the *Jesus Calling* devotional that relate to the themes of the Bible passages. In this way, you will learn how to better make space in your life for the Spirit of God to speak to you through the Word of God and the people of God.

THE FLOW OF EACH SESSION

Each session of this study guide contains the following elements:

- CONSIDER IT. The one or two questions in this opening section serve as an icebreaker to help you start to think about the theme of the session. These questions will help you connect the theme to your own past or present experience and will help you get to know the others in your group more deeply. If you've had a busy day and your mind is full of distractions, this section will help you better focus.

- EXPERIENCE IT. Here you will find two readings from *Jesus Calling* along with some questions for reflection. This is your chance to talk with others about the biblical principles within the *Jesus Calling* devotions. Can you relate to what each reading describes? What insights from God's Word does it illuminate? What does it motivate you to do? This section will help you apply these biblical principles to your everyday habits.

- STUDY IT. Next you'll explore one or two Scripture passages connected to the session topic and the readings from *Jesus Calling*. You will not only analyze these passages but also pray through them in ways designed to engage your heart as well as your head. You'll first talk with your group about what the passage means and then spend several minutes in silence, letting God speak into your own life through His Word.

- LIVE IT. Finally, you will find five days' worth of suggested Scripture passages that you can pray through on your own during the week. Suggested questions for additional study and reflection are provided.

FOR LEADERS

If you are leading a group through this study guide, please see the Leader's Notes at the end of the guide. You'll find background on the design of the study as well as suggested answers for some of the study questions.

A LIFE OF REJOICING

CONSIDER IT

Worship is not just something we do for an hour a week at church. It is something God invites us to do all day long as we go through our lives at home, at work, alone, and with anyone we encounter. The more aware we are of God, the more worship threads itself through the fabric of our lives. There are a number of habits that make up all-day worship, and in this first session we will look at the habit of rejoicing. In particular, what is rejoicing, and how do we weave it into our lives?

1. *When you were growing up, what role (if any) did rejoicing in God or life play in your family?*

_____

_____

_____

_____

EXPERIENCE IT

"Come to Me with a thankful heart, so that you can enjoy My Presence. This is the day that I have made. I want you to rejoice *today*, refusing to worry about tomorrow. Search for all that I have prepared for you, anticipating abundant blessings and accepting difficulties as they come. I can weave miracles into the most mundane day if you keep your focus on Me. Come to Me with all your needs, knowing that *My glorious riches are a more-than-adequate supply.* Stay in continual communication with Me, so that you can live above your circumstances even while you are in the midst of them. *Present your requests to Me with thanksgiving, and My Peace, which surpasses all comprehension, will guard your heart and mind.*"

—FROM *JESUS CALLING*, JANUARY 17

2. *What reasons do we have for rejoicing today?*

3. *What does rejoicing look like for you? What actions, words, and attitudes does it involve?*

"*Rejoice in Me always!* No matter what is going on, you can rejoice in your Love-relationship with Me. This is *the secret of being content in all circumstances.* So many people dream of the day when they will finally be happy: when they are out of debt, when their children are out of trouble, when they have more leisure time, and so on. While they daydream, their moments are trickling into the ground like precious balm spilling wastefully from overturned bottles. Fantasizing about future happiness will never bring fulfillment, because fantasy is unreality. Even though I am invisible, I am far more Real than the world you see around you. My reality is eternal and unchanging. Bring your moments to Me, and I will fill them with vibrant Joy. *Now* is the time to rejoice in My Presence!"

—From *Jesus Calling*, September 11

4. *Why should we rejoice in our relationship with Jesus? What reasons can you think of?*

_____

_____

_____

_____

5. *Why is rejoicing in Jesus better than dreaming of the day when we will be happy?*

_____

_____

_____

_____

STUDY IT

Read aloud the following passage from Philippians 4:4–9. In these verses, the apostle Paul gives wise counsel to a community of believers in the city of Philippi. Paul is writing from prison, and his Philippian readers have also been through difficult circumstances, including discrimination from their neighbors because of their faith.

> Rejoice in the Lord always. I will say it again: Rejoice! Let your gentleness be evident to all. The Lord is near. Do not be anxious about anything, but in every situation, by prayer and petition, with thanksgiving, present your requests to God. And the peace of God, which transcends all understanding, will guard your hearts and your minds in Christ Jesus.

Finally, brothers and sisters, whatever is true, whatever is noble, whatever is right, whatever is pure, whatever is lovely, whatever is admirable—if anything is excellent or praiseworthy—think about such things. Whatever you have learned or received or heard from me, or seen in me—put it into practice. And the God of peace will be with you.

6. *What does it mean to rejoice "in the Lord"? How is that different from just positive thinking or having an upbeat mood?*

7. *Anxiety can make it hard for us to rejoice. What alternative to anxiety does Paul advise us to practice? Why is Paul's advice more effective than worry?*

8. *How does filling your mind with what is true, noble, right, pure, lovely, and admirable help to foster joy?*

9. *When you think about what Paul tells us to fill our minds with, what are the implications for the things we choose to watch on television and the Internet, the games we play, the music we listen to, and the other media we consume?*

10. *Read the passage aloud again. Take two minutes of silence to reread the passage, looking for a sentence, phrase, or even one word that stands out as something Jesus wants you to hear. Ask Him to help you hear Him. If you're meeting with a group, the leader will keep track of time. At the end of two minutes, you may share with the group the word or phrase that came to you in the silence.*

11. *Read the passage aloud again. Take two minutes of silence, asking Jesus what He is saying to you through the word or phrase you selected and whether He would like you to do anything in response. If you're meeting with a group, the leader will again keep track of time. At the end of two minutes, you may share with the group what came to you in the silence if you wish.*

12. *What was it like for you to sit in silence with the passage? Did soaking in the passage like this help you take it in better than before?*

_____

_____

_____

_____

13. *If you're meeting with a group, how can the members pray for you? If you're using this study on your own, what would you like to say to God right now?*

_____

_____

_____

_____

LIVE IT

At the end of each session you'll find suggested Scripture readings for spending time alone with God during five days of the coming week. Each day of this week's readings deal with the theme of rejoicing. Read the passage slowly, pausing to think about what is being said. Rather than approaching this as an assignment to complete, think of it as an opportunity to meet with a Person. Use any of the questions that are helpful.

Day 1

Read Habakkuk 3:17–18. How does Habakkuk describe his circumstances?

_____

_____

_____

_____

What would be some parallel circumstances you might face?

_____

_____

_____

_____

How do you think it's possible for Habakkuk to rejoice in the Lord given the circumstances he is facing? If things are this bad, in what sense is God his Savior?

_____

_____

_____

_____

How easy is it for you to have Habakkuk's attitude? Why?

_____

_____

_____

Spend some time rejoicing in the Lord.

Day 2

Read 1 Thessalonians 5:16–18. Here again we have the connection between rejoicing, praying continually, and giving thanks. Why is rejoicing an essential element of prayer? How is it linked to gratitude?

_____

_____

_____

For what can you give thanks today? What do you want to ask from God?

_____

_____

_____

How can you rejoice in Him even as you ask Him for what you need and thank Him for caring for you?

_____

_____

_____

_____

Day 3

Read Psalm 5:11–12. What does the psalmist ask for? How will that lead to joy?

_____

_____

_____

_____

What blessings has the Lord given you? How is He protecting you?

_____

_____

_____

_____

What protection do you need from God today?

_____

_____

_____

_____

Go to the Lord with gladness and express your needs to Him. How can you rejoice in Him today?

_____

_____

_____

_____

Day 4

Read Psalm 13:1–6. What emotions does the psalmist express in verses 1–3? What does he ask for?

_____

_____

_____

In the midst of these emotions and requests, the psalmist says, "My heart rejoices in your salvation." How is it possible for him to rejoice in his salvation in the midst of his needs and questions?

How can you rejoice in your salvation in the midst of your needs and questions?

What are your questions? What are your needs? Can you say, like the psalmist, "he has been good to me"?

Express your needs and questions to the Lord in the context of rejoicing in your salvation.

Day 5

Read Psalm 16:5–11. What does it mean to say the Lord is your "portion"? How is He the cup you have been given to drink?

_____

_____

_____

_____

What is the inheritance from the Lord that every Christian can delight in?

_____

_____

_____

_____

Why does the psalmist rejoice? Can you rejoice for the same reasons?

_____

_____

_____

_____

Praise God for the eternal pleasures you have already begun to experience with Him and will experience even more in the future.

A Life of
Thankfulness

CONSIDER IT

"The Lord is near" (Philippians 4:5). That alone is reason for us to rejoice! And closely linked to joy is gratitude. These are states of mind we can choose to cultivate by choosing what we think about, dwell on, and fill our heads with. We are not slaves of circumstance. No matter what is happening around us, we can decide to take on thankfulness as a practice that strengthens our souls. In this session we'll look at reasons for thankfulness as well as its results.

1. *Name three things you are thankful for. How easy was it for you to think of these three?*

_____

_____

_____

_____

EXPERIENCE IT

"Thankfulness opens the door to My Presence. Though I am always with you, I have gone to great measures to preserve your freedom of choice. I have placed a door between you and Me, and I have empowered you to open or close that door. There are many ways to open it, but a grateful attitude is one of the most effective. Thankfulness is built on a substructure of trust. When thankful words stick in your throat, you need to check up on your foundation of trust. When thankfulness flows freely from your heart and lips, let your gratitude draw you closer to Me. I want you to learn the art of *giving thanks in all circumstances.* See how many times you can thank Me daily; this will awaken your awareness to a multitude of blessings. It will also cushion the impact of trials when they come against you. Practice My Presence by practicing the discipline of thankfulness."

—FROM *JESUS CALLING*, JULY 24

2. *What is the role of thankfulness in a relationship? How does thankfulness help open the door to God's Presence?*

3. *What is the connection between thankfulness and trust? Where do you see that at work in your own life?*

"A thankful attitude opens windows of heaven. Spiritual blessings fall freely onto you through those openings into eternity. Moreover, as you look up with a grateful heart, you get glimpses of Glory through those windows. You cannot yet live in heaven, but you can experience foretastes of your ultimate home. Such samples of heavenly fare revive your hope. Thankfulness opens you up to these experiences, which then provide further reasons to be grateful. Thus, your path becomes an upward spiral: ever increasing in gladness. Thankfulness is not some sort of magic formula; it is the language of Love, which enables you to communicate intimately with Me. A thankful mindset does not entail a denial of reality with its plethora of problems. Instead, it *rejoices in Me, your Savior*, in the midst of trials and tribulations. *I am your refuge and strength, an ever-present and well-proved help in trouble.*"

—FROM *JESUS CALLING*, NOVEMBER 22

4. *What are some of the benefits of thankfulness? Have you experienced any of these? If so, explain.*

5. *What is the difference between being thankful in spite of your circumstances and being in denial of your problems?*

STUDY IT

Read aloud the following passage from Luke 17:11–19. Jesus goes into a mostly Jewish village, but at least one man there is a Samaritan. The Samaritans were part Jewish and part pagan, and so the Jews regarded them as ethnic and religious half-breeds. Relations between them were often hostile. "Leprosy" refers to a group of skin diseases, some of which were highly contagious and fatal, so lepers were cast out of regular society. They were considered "unclean" both religiously and socially. Priests served as the health inspectors who could certify that someone was cured or "cleansed" of leprosy and therefore "clean" for social contact.

Now on his way to Jerusalem, Jesus traveled along the border between Samaria and Galilee. As he was going into a village, ten men who had leprosy met him. They stood at a distance and called out in a loud voice, "Jesus, Master, have pity on us!"

When he saw them, he said, "Go, show yourselves to the priests." And as they went, they were cleansed.

One of them, when he saw he was healed, came back, praising God in a loud voice. He threw himself at Jesus' feet and thanked him—and he was a Samaritan.

Jesus asked, "Were not all ten cleansed? Where are the other nine? Has no one returned to give praise to God except this foreigner?" Then he said to him, "Rise and go; your faith has made you well."

6. *Which surprises you more: the behavior of the nine who went to the priests or the behavior of the one who went back to thank Jesus? Why?*

----

7. *All ten of them were cleansed, so why does Jesus say of the Samaritan, "your faith has made you well"? In what sense was he made well in a way the other nine might not have been?*

----

8. *The Jewish hearers of this story would have been ashamed that the grateful one was a Samaritan, a foreigner who didn't know God the way Jewish people did. If this story were happening in your world, what "foreign" group would the Samaritan belong to? What type of person would be the last person you would expect to see rushing back to thank God?*

_____

_____

_____

_____

9. *How easy is it for you to practice thankfulness as you go through your day? Rate yourself on a scale of 1 to 5. Why do you think this is the case with you?*

1	2	3	4	5
I have a hard time being thankful.			Thankfulness comes easily to me.	

10. *What helps you practice thankfulness? What gets in the way?*

_____

_____

_____

_____

_____

11. *Read the passage aloud again. Take two minutes of silence to reread the passage, looking for a sentence, phrase, or even one word that stands out as something Jesus wants you to hear. Ask Him to help you hear Him. If you're meeting with a group, the leader will keep track of time. At the end of two minutes, you may share with the group the word or phrase that came to you in the silence.*

---

12. *Read the passage aloud again. Take two minutes of silence, asking Jesus what He is saying to you through the word or phrase you selected and whether He would like you to do anything in response. If you're meeting with a group, the leader will again keep track of time. At the end of two minutes, you may share with the group what came to you in the silence if you wish.*

---

13. *If you're meeting with a group, how can the members pray for you? If you're using this study on your own, what would you like to say to God right now?*

LIVE IT

The theme of this week's daily Scripture readings is thankfulness. Read each passage slowly, pausing to think about what is being said. Rather than approaching this as an assignment to complete, think of it as an opportunity to meet with a Person. Use any of the questions that are helpful.

Day 1

Read Psalm 69:29–33. What is the psalmist's situation? What sort of salvation do you think he is asking for?

How does thanksgiving in such a situation glorify God? Why do you think the Lord is more pleased with thanksgiving than with sacrifice?

_____

_____

_____

_____

How does thanksgiving affect others who hear you offering it? How does this psalm motivate you to thank God?

_____

_____

_____

_____

Offer God your prayers and your thanks.

Day 2

Read 1 Thessalonians 5:18. What do you think it means to give thanks "in all circumstances"? How is that possible?

_____

_____

_____

_____

*Is there a difference between giving thanks **in** a circumstance and giving thanks **for** it? What is that difference?*

_____

_____

_____

_____

Are there any circumstances in your life you find it hard to give thanks in? Why do you think this is God's will for you? How does it strengthen you?

_____

_____

_____

_____

Make a list of things you are thankful for in the midst of your current circumstances. Read it to God.

Day 3

Read Psalm 100. What does this psalm say about God?

_____

_____

_____

_____

What does it mean that God's people are "the sheep of his pasture"? Why is that something to be thankful for?

_____

_____

_____

Are you thankful that God made you? Why or why not?

_____

_____

_____

How does God show His faithfulness to you?

_____

_____

_____

Pray this psalm back to the Lord, personalizing it with your own words.

Day 4

Read Psalm 107:1–9. The psalmist says, "Let the redeemed of the LORD tell their story." How does your story reflect the Lord's goodness and love?

_____

_____

_____

_____

What is the story of the people described in verses 4–9? In what ways can you identify with them? In what ways is your story different?

_____

_____

_____

_____

Have you cried out to the Lord in your trouble? If not, do so now. Who would benefit from hearing your grateful story of redemption?

_____

_____

_____

_____

Day 5

Read Psalm 107:10–16. What is the story of the people described here? Why should they be thankful?

_____

_____

_____

_____

In what ways can you identify with them? In what ways is your story different?

_____

_____

_____

_____

Have you been saved from your distress yet, or are you still waiting? What can you thank God for today, even if He hasn't finished rescuing you yet?

_____

_____

_____

_____

What are His wonderful deeds for humankind?

_____

_____

_____

_____

A LIFE OF CONFESSION AND FORGIVENESS

CONSIDER IT

A life of worship includes dealing with the sins that come between us and God. Some people tend to be acutely aware of their faults and feel guilt easily, while others tend to be unaware of their faults and don't naturally feel much guilt. This is a difference of personality; neither type is necessarily more sinful than the other. Those who are acutely aware will benefit by not getting bogged down in small mistakes and genuinely letting go of self-blame after they admit their wrongdoings to God. Those who tend to be more unaware will benefit by making time each day to examine themselves and ask God to show them what they've done wrong. In this session, we'll look at the benefits of regular self-examination and confession.

1. *How would you rate yourself on your awareness of your faults?*

1	2	3	4	5

I tend to be blind when it comes
to my faults.

I tend to be acutely aware
and blame myself a lot.

EXPERIENCE IT

"When your sins weigh heavily upon you, come to Me. Confess your wrongdoing, which I know all about before you say a word. Stay in the Light of My Presence, receiving forgiveness, cleansing, and healing. Remember that I have clothed *you in My righteousness*, so nothing can separate you from Me. Whenever you stumble or fall, I am there to help you up. Man's tendency is to hide from his sin, seeking refuge in the darkness. There he indulges in self-pity, denial, self-righteousness, blaming, and hatred. But *I am the Light of the world*, and My illumination decimates the darkness. Come close to Me and let My Light envelop you, driving out darkness and permeating you with Peace."

—FROM *JESUS CALLING*, MAY 20

2. *What encouragement do we have for confessing our sins?*

_____

_____

_____

_____

3. *Hiding from sin leads to self-pity, denial, self-righteousness, blaming, and hatred. What are some examples of how each of these problems might be connected to us hiding from our sin? (For instance, if we have a fight with someone and don't want to admit our sin is partly to blame, we might blame the other person for causing the fight.)*

_____

_____

_____

_____

"Walk with Me in the freedom of forgiveness. The path we follow together is sometimes steep and slippery. If you carry a burden of guilt on your back, you are more likely to stumble and fall. At your request, I will remove the heavy load from you and bury it at the foot of the cross. When I unburden you, you are undeniably free! Stand up straight and tall in My Presence, so that no one can place more burdens on your back. Look into My Face and feel the warmth of My Love-Light shining upon you. It is this unconditional Love that frees you from both fears and sins. Spend time basking in the Light of My Presence. As you come to know Me more and more intimately, you grow increasingly free."

—FROM *JESUS CALLING*, SEPTEMBER 23

4. *How does a burden of guilt cause a person to stumble? In other words, how does it lead a person either to sin or to be unwilling to keep going with Jesus?*

_____

_____

_____

_____

5. *How easy is it for you to walk in the freedom of forgiveness? Why? Are you weighed down by unconfessed sin, or do you need to stop carrying around the memories of old sins that have been confessed and forgiven?*

_____

_____

_____

_____

STUDY IT

Read aloud the following passage from Psalm 32:1–5.

> Blessed is the one
>> whose transgressions are forgiven,
>> whose sins are covered.
> Blessed is the one
>> whose sin the LORD does not count against them
>> and in whose spirit is no deceit.

When I kept silent,
>   my bones wasted away
>   through my groaning all day long.
> For day and night
>   your hand was heavy on me;
> my strength was sapped
>   as in the heat of summer.
> Then I acknowledged my sin to you
>   and did not cover up my iniquity.
> I said, "I will confess
>   my transgressions to the Lord."
> And you forgave
>   the guilt of my sin.

6. *The psalmist says his strength was sapped because "day and night [the Lord's] hand was heavy on me." What does this mean?*

_____

_____

_____

_____

7. *What are the blessings of forgiveness? How is life better when we are forgiven?*

_____

_____

_____

_____

8. *If forgiveness is so blessed, why do you think people so often avoid asking for it? What is hard about confession?*

_____

_____

_____

_____

_____

_____

9. *First John 1:8–9 states, "If we claim to be without sin, we deceive ourselves and the truth is not in us. If we confess our sins, [God] is faithful and just and will forgive us our sins." Have you ever felt your sins were too bad for God to forgive? How does John address that feeling in this passage?*

_____

_____

_____

_____

_____

10. *In Psalm 139:23–24, David writes, "Search me, God, and know my heart; test me and know my anxious thoughts. See if there is any offensive way in me, and lead me in the way everlasting." Some people find it beneficial to set a time during the day (such as in the evening or first thing in the morning) to review the past twenty-four hours and ask God to search their hearts for any sins to confess. Some stop what they are doing the instant they recognize they have fallen into sin and confess what they've done. Others find it helpful to talk to a trusted friend about any sin patterns that person recognizes in their lives. What benefits do you see with each of these practices? What do you think would be the most helpful way for you to build confession into your routine?*

11. *Read Psalm 32:1–5 aloud again. Take two minutes of silence to reread the passage, looking for a sentence, phrase, or even one word that stands out as something Jesus wants you to hear. Ask Him to help you hear Him. If you're meeting with a group, the leader will keep track of time. At the end of two minutes, you may share with the group the word or phrase that came to you in the silence.*

12. *Read Psalm 32:1–5 aloud again. Take two minutes of silence, asking Jesus what He is saying to you through the word or phrase you selected and whether He would like you to do anything in response. If you're meeting with a group, the leader will again keep track of time. At the end of two minutes, you may share with the group what came to you in the silence if you wish.*

13. *If you're meeting with a group, how can the members pray for you? If you're using this study on your own, what would you like to say to God right now?*

LIVE IT

The theme of this week's daily Scripture readings is confession and forgiveness. Read each passage slowly, pausing to think about what is being said. Rather than approaching this as an assignment to complete, think of it as an opportunity to meet with a Person. Use any of the questions that are helpful.

Day 1

Read Psalm 32:8–11. What do verses 8–11 have to do with the theme of confession and forgiveness that David wrote about in verses 1–5?

Why are these verses a natural follow-up to acknowledging what we've done wrong and wanting to live differently?

What do these verses tell us about how to live differently and overcome our habitual sins?

When have you been like a "mule" when it comes to something the Lord wanted you to do?

Are you currently being mulish about any area of your life? If so, confess that honestly and decide to do what you know you should. Rejoice in the Lord's forgiveness and guidance for living a godly life.

Day 2

Read Psalm 51:1–4. Why can we hope for mercy from God when we acknowledge our sins? How is mercy different from saying that wrong behavior doesn't matter or isn't really wrong?

Notice the psalmist asks God to wash away his iniquities. Why is this a good picture of what we need when we have sinned?

Why does the psalmist say "against you [God] have I sinned," even when he has harmed a human being?

Thank God for His unfailing love and compassion for you and confess any sins that are on your heart.

Day 3

Read Psalm 51:7–12. Can God literally hide His face from our sins? What is the psalmist asking for here?

What does the psalmist ask for in verse 10 that goes beyond just forgiveness?

_____

_____

_____

Why is it important to have a changed heart and spirit? How does forgiveness lead to the joy of salvation?

_____

_____

_____

How does sin cut us off from the joy of salvation?

_____

_____

_____

What is a willing spirit, and why do we need it?

_____

_____

_____

_____

Pray this passage back to God, focusing on those parts that you most long for.

Day 4

Read Psalm 51:13–17. What will the psalmist do when God has granted him forgiveness and a spirit willing to do what is right? Why does he want to do that?

_____

_____

_____

_____

Why does forgiveness lead the psalmist to praise? What kind of worship offering does the Lord desire from us?

_____

_____

_____

_____

What does the psalmist mean when he writes, "My sacrifice, O God, is a broken spirit"? Why would the Lord desire that?

Spend some time praising God for the forgiveness and cleansing He gives you.

Day 5

Read 1 John 3:16–18. Describe the love John asks us to practice here.

What opportunities does your life give for practicing this kind of love? When have you missed an opportunity to do so?

Sometimes we need God's forgiveness for the things we should do but haven't done. Talk with God about any ways you fall short of love. Is there some area in which you need forgiveness and a fresh start?

_____

_____

_____

_____

Ask God to enable you to love the people around you with actions and truth.

A LIFE FREE FROM IDOLS

CONSIDER IT

A life of worshiping the one true God is also a life free from the worship of false gods. False worship can mean dabbling in other religions and spiritualties, but often it is as simple as treating any person or thing as the source of our life. An idol is *anyone or anything we love more than God or fear more than God*. Maybe we think and act as if our life depends on some particular person. Maybe money or the lack of it has us in the grip of fear or desire. In this session, we'll look at those things we tend to love or fear more than God and see if we can knock them off the pedestal only God should occupy.

1. *We know life depends on God, but what types of things tend to tempt you to put something else in His place?*

_____

_____

_____

_____

EXPERIENCE IT

"I am the Risen One who shines upon you always. You worship a living Deity, not some idolatrous, man-made image. Your relationship with Me is meant to be vibrant and challenging, as I invade more and more areas of your life. Do not fear change, for I am making you a *new creation, with old things passing away and new things continually on the horizon*. When you cling to old ways and sameness, you resist My work within you. I want you to embrace all that I am doing in your life, finding your security in Me alone. It is easy to make an idol of routine, finding security within the boundaries you build around your life. Although each day contains twenty-four hours, every single one presents a unique set of circumstances. Don't try to force-fit today into yesterday's mold. Instead, ask Me to open your eyes, so you can find all I have prepared for you in this precious day of Life."

—FROM *JESUS CALLING*, FEBRUARY 17

2. *Do you fear change? What is the evidence you do or don't?*

3. *What makes you feel secure? What makes you feel insecure?*

"Worship Me only. Idolatry has always been the downfall of My people. I make no secrets about being *a jealous God*. Current idols are more subtle than ancient ones, because today's false gods are often outside the field of religion. People, possessions, status, and self-aggrandizement are some of the most popular deities today. Beware of bowing down before these things. False gods never satisfy; instead, they stir up lust for more and more. When you seek Me instead of the world's idols, you experience My Joy and Peace. These intangibles slake the thirst of your soul, providing deep satisfaction. The glitter of the world is tinny and temporal. The Light of My Presence is brilliant and everlasting. Walk in the Light with Me. Thus you become a beacon through whom others are drawn to Me."

—FROM *JESUS CALLING*, JULY 11

4. *What would be the signs a person is treating status as a god? What would be the signs a person is treating some other individual as a god?*

_____

_____

_____

_____

5. *Why is it both safe and wise to let go of false gods?*

_____

_____

_____

STUDY IT

Read aloud the following passage from Exodus 20:2–5. This is the beginning of a longer passage in which God gives the Ten Commandments to Moses.

> "I am the LORD your God, who brought you out of Egypt, out of the land of slavery.
>
> "You shall have no other gods before me.
>
> "You shall not make for yourself an image in the form of anything in heaven above or on the earth beneath or in the waters below. You shall not bow down to them or worship them; for I, the LORD your God, am a jealous God."

6. *God's command to have no other gods before Him is rooted in the first sentence in this passage: "I am the Lord your God, who brought you out of . . . slavery." What form of bondage and slavery has God rescued you from? How significant is it to be released from sin? Why?*

---

7. *What does God mean when He calls Himself "jealous"? Why is He legitimately jealous of our affections?*

---

8. *In Matthew 6:24, Jesus says, "No one can serve two masters; for either he will hate the one and love the other, or else he will be loyal to the one and despise the other. You cannot serve God and mammon" (NKJV).* **Mammon** *is a Greek word for material greed or wealth that was often personified as a false god. Why is it impossible to serve both God and anything or anyone else?*

---

9. *What is it about money that makes it such an attractive god? Why do we so easily tend to feel our lives depend on money?*

10. *Why should we depend on God rather than material wealth?*

11. *Read the passage aloud again. Take two minutes of silence to reread the passage, looking for a sentence, phrase, or even one word that stands out as something Jesus wants you to hear. Ask Him to help you hear Him. If you're meeting with a group, the leader will keep track of time. At the end of two minutes, you may share with the group the word or phrase that came to you in the silence.*

12. *Read the passage aloud again. Take two minutes of silence, asking Jesus what He is saying to you through the word or phrase you selected and whether He would like you to do anything in response. If you're meeting with a group, the leader will again keep track of time. At the end of two minutes, you may share with the group what came to you in the silence if you wish.*

13. *If you're meeting with a group, how can the members pray for you? If you're using this study on your own, what would you like to say to God right now?*

LIVE IT

The theme of this week's daily Scripture readings is rejecting idols. Read each passage slowly, pausing to think about what is being said. Rather than approaching this as an assignment to complete, think of it as an opportunity to meet with a Person. Use any of the questions that are helpful.

Day 1

Read Isaiah 40:18–22. Why can't we compare God to an idol? How much bigger is He?

How are our idols today like those made of metal or wood? How are they different?

Can technology or other things we make become idols? What are the signs that something man-made has become an idol to us?

Talk with God about something you are tempted to put in His place as a perceived source of life. Ask Him to help you know how much bigger and more dependable He is.

Day 2

Read Isaiah 45:18–21. Three times in these verses the Lord says there is no other God but Him. Why do you think He repeats that?

_____

_____

_____

_____

What is the allure of other gods?

_____

_____

_____

The Lord says, "I have not spoken in secret." How have you experienced the truth of this? Why do some people feel like the Lord speaks in secret?

_____

_____

_____

_____

The Lord also says, "I have not said to Jacob's descendants, 'Seek me in vain.'" How have you experienced that seeking Him is valuable and gets you somewhere?

Spend some time seeking God and asking Him for the things you most need.

Day 3

Read Romans 1:20–23. What are God's invisible qualities? How does the created world make them visible?

Why don't people see the Creator's hand in created things?

What does it mean to have one's thinking become futile? Do you think it's possible to reject God and worship nothing, or does everybody worship something?

Give God praise for His eternal power, His divine nature, and the way He makes those things known to you in His creation.

Day 4

Read Psalm 24:1–6. Why does the whole earth belong to the Lord? How is that a powerful reason to reject idols?

Verse 4 refers to an idol as "what is false" (ESV). What are the false things in which you are tempted to place your trust? What blessings do they falsely promise?

What blessings does the Lord truly promise?

_____

_____

_____

Worship the Lord as your Creator and ask Him to draw your heart away from false things and toward Him. Thank Him for the many blessings He gives you.

Day 5

Read Psalm 36:5–12. What reasons for trusting the Lord rather than idols does this passage offer? Which reason speaks most deeply to you today?

_____

_____

_____

_____

How do you need God's justice? How do you need His faithfulness?

_____

_____

_____

_____

What is the river of delights that God offers?

_____

_____

_____

_____

Pray this passage back to God, personalizing it for your situation. Ask the Lord to help you trust Him rather than the false things you're tempted to trust.

A LIFE OF SEEKING GOD'S THOUGHTS

CONSIDER IT

The Lord is much, much bigger than we are. That's good news, because it means He's much, much bigger than our needs and our problems. It also means, however, that His thoughts and plans are often beyond our imagining. When we're locked into our own thoughts, He invites us to read His Word and discover His thoughts. He invites us to pray and ask for guidance that we wouldn't think of on our own. A life of worship stretches us beyond ourselves. In this session, we'll consider what it means to truly seek God's thoughts.

1. *What is your typical attitude toward planning? Are you the kind of person who likes to plan ahead in detail? Do you make general plans for your day? Or do you prefer to be more spontaneous?*

EXPERIENCE IT

"Come to Me with your plans held in abeyance. *Worship Me in spirit and in truth*, allowing My Glory to permeate your entire being. Trust Me enough to let Me guide you through this day, accomplishing My purposes in My timing. Subordinate your myriad plans to My Master Plan. I am sovereign over every aspect of your life! The challenge continually before you is to trust Me and search for My way through each day. Do not blindly follow your habitual route, or you will miss what I have prepared for you. *As the heavens are higher than the earth, so are My ways higher than your ways and My thoughts than your thoughts.*"

—FROM *JESUS CALLING*, MAY 18

2. *What attitude should we have toward planning? Is planning bad or useless? Why or why not?*

_____

_____

_____

_____

3. *How would you go about searching for God's way to guide you through a day?*

_____

_____

_____

_____

"Thankfulness takes the sting out of adversity. That is why I have instructed you to *give thanks for everything*. There is an element of mystery in this transaction: You give Me thanks (regardless of your feelings), and I give you Joy (regardless of your circumstances). This is a spiritual act of obedience—at times, blind obedience. To people who don't know Me intimately, it can seem irrational and even impossible to thank Me for heartrending hardships. Nonetheless, those who obey Me in this way are invariably blessed, even though difficulties may remain. Thankfulness opens your heart to My Presence and your mind to My thoughts. You may still be in the same place, with the same set of circumstances, but it is as if a light has been switched on, enabling you to see from My perspective. It is this *Light of My Presence* that removes the sting from adversity."

—FROM *JESUS CALLING*, NOVEMBER 24

4. *What does thankfulness do for us?*

_____

_____

_____

_____

5. *How does thankfulness open our minds to God's thoughts and change our thinking to God's way of thinking?*

_____

_____

_____

_____

STUDY IT

Read aloud the following passage from Isaiah 55:6–11.

> Seek the LORD while he may be found;
> > call on him while he is near.
> Let the wicked forsake their ways
> > and the unrighteous their thoughts.
> Let them turn to the LORD, and he will have mercy on them,
> > and to our God, for he will freely pardon.
> "For my thoughts are not your thoughts,
> > neither are your ways my ways,"
> > > declares the LORD.

"As the heavens are higher than the earth,
    so are my ways higher than your ways
    and my thoughts than your thoughts.
As the rain and the snow
    come down from heaven,
and do not return to it
    without watering the earth
and making it bud and flourish,
    so that it yields seed for the sower and bread for the eater,
so is my word that goes out from my mouth:
    It will not return to me empty,
but will accomplish what I desire
    and achieve the purpose for which I sent it."

6. *What does it mean to "seek the Lord"? How do we do that?*

7. *What are some of the ways God's thoughts are higher than ours? Give some examples.*

8. *Think of a situation in your life. What would getting **your** way look like in that circumstance?*

9. *What might it look like for God to get **His** way in that circumstance? What do you think God's desires and purposes might be? If you don't know, how do you deal with not knowing?*

10. *What does Isaiah 55:6–11 promise about God's desires and purposes? How is that important to you personally?*

11. *Read the passage aloud again. Take two minutes of silence to reread the passage, looking for a sentence, phrase, or even one word that stands out as something Jesus wants you to hear. Ask Him to help you hear Him. If you're meeting with a group, the leader will keep track of time. At the end of two minutes, you may share with the group the word or phrase that came to you in the silence.*

12. *Read the passage aloud again. Take two minutes of silence, asking Jesus what He is saying to you through the word or phrase you selected and whether He would like you to do anything in response. If you're meeting with a group, the leader will again keep track of time. At the end of two minutes, you may share with the group what came to you in the silence if you wish.*

13. *If you're meeting with a group, how can the members pray for you? If you're using this study on your own, what would you like to say to God right now?*

LIVE IT

The theme of this week's Scripture readings is seeking God's surprising thoughts. Read each passage slowly, pausing to think about what is being said. Rather than approaching this as an assignment to complete, think of it as an opportunity to meet with a Person. Use any of the questions that are helpful.

Day 1

Read Psalm 119:9–16. What is our prime source for seeking God's thoughts? What benefits of this source does this passage offer?

Why do you suppose the psalmist recounts God's thoughts with his lips? How is that helpful?

_____

_____

_____

How would you go about putting that into practice? How would you hide God's thoughts in your heart? What are the benefits of doing that?

_____

_____

_____

Praise God for making His thoughts available to you.

Day 2

Read Luke 6:20–26. These are words from Jesus. How are the thoughts He is expressing in this passage surprising? How are they higher than most people's thoughts?

_____

_____

_____

Which thought is the most surprising for you? Why that one?

What difference do these thoughts make to your life and your choices?

In what ways do you identify with the people Jesus says are blessed? In what ways do you identify with the ones to whom He says "woe"?

What does "woe" mean to you? Why do these people get Jesus' warning?

Thank Jesus for His promises to you.

Day 3

Read Luke 6:27–31. What is surprising about these thoughts from Jesus? How are they higher than the way most people think?

Jesus practiced what He preached, yet He was crucified by the people He came to love. What does this say about this way of life He is advocating?

Do you think Jesus' words in this passage are practical? Why or why not?

How can this way of life spring from inner strength? How can you put these thoughts into practice?

_____

_____

_____

Ask Jesus to take care of you as you seek to live by His words.

Day 4

Read Luke 6:32–36. What is surprising about these thoughts from Jesus? How are they higher than the way most people think?

_____

_____

_____

What reasons for loving our enemies does Jesus give in these verses? What are the risks of doing this? Why are the risks worth it?

_____

_____

_____

Who is someone in your life who is ungrateful or hard to love? How do you think Jesus would have you treat that person? How can you do good to that person in a way that doesn't give him or her license to do evil?

Ask Jesus to show you how to be wise and loving toward that person.

Day 5

Read Matthew 20:1–16. In this story from Jesus, what is surprising about the way the landowner treats his employees? How do the characters react to his surprising behavior?

What is the point of the story? What does it tell us about how God treats us?

Jesus says, "So the last will be first, and the first will be last." What does that mean to you?

Note that the story doesn't say we should be like the landowner, but it does tell us how we should view people who wait until the last minute to start serving God. How should we view them?

Do you think God's generosity encourages people to be lazy? Why or why not?

Thank God for His generosity to you in inviting you to work in His vineyard.

A LIFE CLOSE
TO GOD

CONSIDER IT

A life of worship is a 24/7 life of intimacy with God. While at first it may be hard for us to think about God during the busyness of the day, as we practice checking in with Him prayerfully, it gets easier to remember Him. Our goal is to go through our days thinking of Him continually—sending up brief prayers of trust, requests for help and guidance, or even just saying His name, "Jesus." When we do, we find He becomes our first thought when we need to solve a problem or thank Him for a blessing. In this session, we'll think about what it means to live close to God and how we can put that into practice.

1. *What are the major distractions in your life that take your mind away from God and the other things you most need to think about?*

_____

_____

_____

EXPERIENCE IT

"Worship Me by living close to Me. This was My original design for man, into whom *I breathed My very breath of Life*. This is My desire for you: that you stay near Me as you walk along your life-path. Each day is an important part of that journey. Although you may feel as if you are going nowhere in this world, your spiritual journey is another matter altogether, taking you along steep, treacherous paths of adventure. That is why *walking in the Light of My Presence* is essential to keep you from stumbling. By staying close to Me, you present yourself as a *living sacrifice*. Even the most routine part of your day can be *a spiritual act of worship, holy and pleasing to Me*."

—FROM *JESUS CALLING*, SEPTEMBER 14

2. *What does living close to God look like in your life?*

_____

_____

_____

_____

_____

3. *What things tend to get in the way of you living close to God?*

_____

_____

_____

_____

_____

"Thank Me in the midst of the crucible. When things seem all wrong, look for growth opportunities. Especially, look for areas where you need to let go, leaving your cares in My able hands. Do you trust Me to orchestrate your life events as I choose, or are you still trying to make things go according to your will? If you keep trying to carry out your intentions while I am leading you in another direction, you deify your desires. Be on the lookout for what I am doing in your life. Worship Me by living close to Me, *thanking Me in all circumstances*."

—FROM *JESUS CALLING*, MAY 13

4. *What is an area in which you need to let go and leave something in Jesus' hands?*

_____

_____

_____

_____

5. *What is one step you could take to live closer to Jesus than you are now?*

_____

_____

_____

_____

STUDY IT

Read aloud the following passage from John 15:1–9. Note that Jesus is speaking.

> "I am the true vine, and my Father is the gardener. He cuts off every branch in me that bears no fruit, while every branch that does bear fruit he prunes so that it will be even more fruitful. You are already clean because of the word I have spoken to you. Remain in me, as I also remain in you. No branch can bear fruit by itself; it must remain in the vine. Neither can you bear fruit unless you remain in me.
>
> "I am the vine; you are the branches. If you remain in me and I in you, you will bear much fruit; apart from me you can do nothing. If

you do not remain in me, you are like a branch that is thrown away and withers; such branches are picked up, thrown into the fire and burned. If you remain in me and my words remain in you, ask whatever you wish, and it will be done for you. This is to my Father's glory, that you bear much fruit, showing yourselves to be my disciples.

"As the Father has loved me, so have I loved you. Now remain in my love. If you keep my commands, you will remain in my love, just as I have kept my Father's commands and remain in his love."

6. *In this passage, Jesus says the Father prunes branches to make them more fruitful. Pruning grape vines means cutting them back so they put more energy into producing fruit and less energy into producing stems and leaves. In what ways does the Father prune us?*

7. *What does it mean in practical terms to "remain" or "abide" (NKJV) in Jesus? How do we go about remaining in Him the way a branch remains in a vine?*

8. *According to this passage, why is it essential that we remain in Jesus?*

9. *What does keeping Jesus' commands have to do with remaining in His love? How do you respond to that connection? Is it surprising? Motivating? Dismaying?*

10. *Jesus says, "Apart from me you can do nothing." Have you ever seen that to be true in your life? If so, describe the situation.*

11. *Read the passage aloud again. Take two minutes of silence to reread the passage, looking for a sentence, phrase, or even one word that stands out as something Jesus wants you to hear. Ask Him to help you hear Him. If you're meeting with a group, the leader will keep track of time. At the end of two minutes, you may share with the group the word or phrase that came to you in the silence.*

_____

_____

_____

_____

12. *Read the passage aloud again. Take two minutes of silence, asking Jesus what He is saying to you through the word or phrase you selected and whether He would like you to do anything in response. If you're meeting with a group, the leader will again keep track of time. At the end of two minutes, you may share with the group what came to you in the silence if you wish.*

_____

_____

_____

_____

13. *If you're meeting with a group, how can the members pray for you? If you're using this study on your own, what would you like to say to God right now?*

_____

_____

_____

_____

_____

LIVE IT

The theme of this week's daily Scripture readings is staying close to God. Read the passage slowly, pausing to think about what is being said. Rather than approaching this as an assignment to complete, think of it as an opportunity to meet with a Person. Use any of the questions that are helpful.

Day 1

Read Psalm 143:5–8. What are some examples of the works of God that are worth meditating on? How does meditating on His works bring us closer to Him?

_____

_____

_____

_____

How great is your thirst for God? How does that thirst affect the way you live? Or, if you don't thirst for Him that much, why do you think that is the case?

_____

_____

_____

_____

What does the psalmist ask God for? What would you like to ask God for? Do any of the psalmist's requests resonate with you?

_____

_____

_____

_____

Pray this passage back to God, personalizing it with your own needs.

Day 2

Read Exodus 13:20–22. In the time of Moses, the Lord led His people by being present with them in a pillar of cloud by day and a pillar of fire by night. What would be the advantages of that kind of guidance?

_____

_____

_____

How does the Lord lead us today? Why do you think He does it differently today?

_____

_____

_____

_____

What guidance do you need today? How can you remain in God today so that you are alert to receive His direction?

_____

_____

_____

_____

Thank the Lord for His willingness to guide you.

Day 3

Read Psalm 119:33–40. What are some of the ways the psalmist says he cultivates closeness with God?

_____

_____

_____

_____

Why is it important to do the things God has commanded?

_____

_____

_____

_____

What are some of God's commands that you know? How does your life give you an opportunity to do them?

_____

_____

_____

_____

If you don't know God's commands, how can you learn them? Do you love God's commands, or do they feel like a burden to you?

_____

_____

_____

_____

Ask God to work in your soul so you are free from the things that hinder you, free to do the things He commands.

Day 4

Read John 15:9–13. How do these words of Jesus urge you to remain or abide in Him? Does it give you joy to keep Jesus' commands?

What command does Jesus single out for mention? Why do you think this command is so essential to living close to Him?

What opportunities do you have for loving others sacrificially? What helps you do that? What gets in the way?

Ask God to show you opportunities today to love others and to empower you to love the way Jesus loves.

Day 5

Read John 15:14–17. What does it mean to be Jesus' friend? How do we live as Jesus' friends?

How does this passage explain the fruit Jesus wants us to bear? Why is this fruit important?

Do you find that love comes naturally when you stay close to Jesus, or do you have to work at it? What opportunities to love have you had in the past couple of days?

_____

_____

_____

_____

Talk with Jesus about the ups and downs of how those situations have gone.

A Life of the Beauty of Holiness

CONSIDER IT

"Worship the Lord in the beauty of holiness! Tremble before Him, all the earth" (Psalm 96:9 NKJV). The phrase "the beauty of holiness" in Scripture has many facets. On the one hand, it suggests holiness is beautiful and the key to growing in beauty is growing more holy—more like Jesus. On the other hand, it suggests beauty matters, because it reflects something of who the holy God is. In this session, we'll explore this phrase and consider how we can worship the Lord in the beauty of holiness.

1. *List three words that you associate with the word* **beauty**. *(For example, "makeup, fashion, trivial" or "majestic, nature, mountains.")*

EXPERIENCE IT

"Worship Me in the beauty of holiness. All true beauty reflects some of who I am. I am working My ways in you: the divine Artist creating loveliness within your being. My main work is to clear out debris and clutter, making room for My Spirit to take full possession. Collaborate with Me in this effort by being willing to let go of anything I choose to take away. I know what you need, and I have promised to provide all of that—abundantly! Your sense of security must not rest in your possessions or in things going your way. I am training you to depend on Me alone, finding fulfillment in My Presence. This entails being satisfied with much or with little, accepting *either* as My will for the moment. Instead of grasping and controlling, you are learning to release and receive. Cultivate this receptive stance by trusting Me in every situation."

—FROM *JESUS CALLING*, NOVEMBER 7

2. *How does God create loveliness within our being? What are some examples of clutter He might want to clear away?*

_____

_____

_____

_____

3. *What is a circumstance in which you need to depend on God alone and not on things going your way?*

_____

_____

_____

_____

"*Worship Me in the beauty of holiness.* I created beauty to declare the existence of My holy Being. A magnificent rose, a hauntingly glorious sunset, oceanic splendor—all these things were meant to proclaim My Presence in the world. Most people rush past these proclamations without giving them a second thought. Some people use beauty, especially feminine loveliness, to sell their products. How precious are My children who are awed by nature's beauty; this opens them up to My holy Presence. Even before you knew Me personally, you responded to My creation with wonder. This is a gift, and it carries responsibility with it. Declare My glorious Being to the world. *The whole earth is full of My radiant beauty—My Glory!*"

—From *Jesus Calling*, July 30

4. *What did you see recently in the natural world that was beautiful? If you can't think of anything, how might you build regular exposure to nature into your life?*

_____

_____

_____

_____

5. *As human beings we are part of the natural world that God created, but all too often we do not see ourselves as His beautiful creations. How can we better see God's beauty in ourselves and in others?*

_____

_____

_____

_____

STUDY IT

Read aloud the following passage from Psalm 96:1–13 (NKJV).

> Oh, sing to the LORD a new song!
> Sing to the LORD, all the earth.
> Sing to the LORD, bless His name;
> Proclaim the good news of His salvation from day to day.
> Declare His glory among the nations,
> His wonders among all peoples.

For the LORD is great and greatly to be praised;
He is to be feared above all gods.
For all the gods of the peoples are idols,
But the LORD made the heavens.
Honor and majesty are before Him;
Strength and beauty are in His sanctuary.

Give to the LORD, O families of the peoples,
Give to the LORD glory and strength.
Give to the LORD the glory due His name;
Bring an offering, and come into His courts.
Oh, worship the LORD in the beauty of holiness!
Tremble before Him, all the earth.

Say among the nations, "The LORD reigns;
The world also is firmly established,
It shall not be moved;
He shall judge the peoples righteously."

Let the heavens rejoice, and let the earth be glad;
Let the sea roar, and all its fullness;
Let the field be joyful, and all that is in it.
Then all the trees of the woods will rejoice before the Lord.
For He is coming, for He is coming to judge the earth.
He shall judge the world with righteousness,
And the peoples with His truth.

6. *According to this psalm, what sets the Lord apart from idols? Why does this make Him infinitely higher than idols?*

7. *"Strength and beauty are in His sanctuary." Why do you think the psalmist looks for strength and beauty in the place where God is worshiped? Is beauty important for a worship space? Why or why not?*

_____

_____

_____

_____

8. *How do you think we "worship the Lord in the beauty of holiness"?*

_____

_____

_____

_____

9. *What does it mean for the heavens, the earth, the sea, the field, and the trees all to join in rejoicing before the Lord? How does the natural world worship Him?*

_____

_____

_____

_____

10. *What is awe? What reasons do we have to feel awe when we enter the Lord's Presence?*

11. *Read the passage aloud again. Take two minutes of silence to reread the passage, looking for a sentence, phrase, or even one word that stands out as something Jesus wants you to hear. Ask Him to help you hear Him. If you're meeting with a group, the leader will keep track of time. At the end of two minutes, you may share with the group the word or phrase that came to you in the silence.*

12. *Read the passage aloud again. Take two minutes of silence, asking Jesus what He is saying to you through the word or phrase you selected and whether He would like you to do anything in response. If you're meeting with a group, the leader will again keep track of time. At the end of two minutes, you may share with the group what came to you in the silence if you wish.*

13. *If you're meeting with a group, how can the members pray for you? If you're using this study on your own, what would you like to say to God right now?*

_____

_____

_____

_____

LIVE IT

The theme of this week's daily Scripture readings is the Lord's beauty and its effect on us. Read each passage slowly, pausing to think about what is being said. Rather than approaching this as an assignment to complete, think of it as an opportunity to meet with a Person. Use any of the questions that are helpful.

Day 1

Read Psalm 19:1–6. How do the heavens (day and night sky) declare the glory of God?

_____

_____

_____

_____

What do the sun, moon, and stars say about God?

Are you moved to praise God when you see the sky? In what ways?

How does contemplating beauty affect the way you see your difficulties?

Today, keep watch for signs of God's glory in the world around you. Ask the Lord to help you notice Him in what He has made.

Day 2

Read Exodus 34:29–35. Why was Moses's face radiant? What do you think that radiance looked like?

How did the radiance affect the people who saw Moses? Why do you think they had that reaction?

What does the radiance tell you about God? What does it tell you about Moses's relationship with God?

How does this passage help you understand the beauty of holiness?

Spend some time in God's Presence, basking in His beauty.

Day 3

Read 2 Corinthians 3:7–9. In verse 7, the apostle Paul refers to Moses's ministry as "the ministry that brought death." Why do you think Paul describes the law brought by Moses in that way?

What is "the ministry of the Spirit"? Why is it more glorious than Moses's ministry?

How does the Spirit's ministry bring righteousness?

_____

_____

_____

_____

Have you ever seen someone radiant with righteousness? If so, what does that look like?

_____

_____

_____

_____

Thank God for the ministry of His Spirit in your life and ask Him to make you radiant with His righteousness.

Day 4

Read 2 Corinthians 3:18. According to this verse, how are we Christians like Moses when he went into the Lord's Presence? How is our situation even better than his?

_____

_____

_____

_____

What does it mean to say we are being transformed into the Lord's image?

How, in practice, do we go about contemplating the Lord's glory? What practices does that involve?

Spend some time in the Lord's Presence, asking Him to show you His glory. Worship Him there.

Day 5

Read Psalm 29:1–9. What does it mean to ascribe glory to the Lord? How do we do that?

What does the psalmist mean when he says the Lord thunders over the waters?

_____

_____

_____

_____

What does the psalmist say about the Lord's voice? What emotions about the Lord do these words evoke in you?

_____

_____

_____

_____

How are you moved to respond? Is this a God to whom you can entrust your needs? Why?

_____

_____

_____

_____

Take some time to worship this thundering, glorious God.

A LIFE OF TENDER
PASSION

CONSIDER IT

If we allow our minds to dwell on the many good things the Lord has done and is doing for us, we are moved to worship. We worship Him not because He requires it, but because He deserves it. The more we turn our minds to dwell on what He has done, the more worship will bubble up from a passionate place in us. In this session, we will encounter the story of one person who expressed her passionate worship in a way that shocked other people but moved Jesus.

1. *What is one thing God has revealed to you during this study on living a life of worship? How are you grateful for that?*

EXPERIENCE IT

"I am the firm foundation on which you can dance and sing and celebrate My Presence. This is My high and holy calling for you; receive it as a precious gift. *Glorifying and enjoying Me* is a higher priority than maintaining a tidy, structured life. Give up your striving to keep everything under control—an impossible task and a waste of precious energy. My guidance for each of My children is unique. That's why listening to Me is so vital for your well-being. Let me prepare you for the day that awaits you and point you in the right direction. I am with you continually, so don't be intimidated by fear. Though it stalks you, it cannot harm you, as long as you cling to My hand. Keep your eyes on Me, enjoying Peace in My Presence."

—FROM *JESUS CALLING*, JUNE 19

2. *Why should glorifying and enjoying God be a higher priority than maintaining a tidy, structured life?*

3. *In what ways can structure be beneficial to our relationship with God? In what ways can it be detrimental?*

"When you worship Me *in spirit and truth*, you join with choirs of angels who are continually before My throne. Though you cannot hear their voices, your praise and thanksgiving are distinctly audible in heaven. Your petitions are also heard, but it is your gratitude that clears the way to My Heart. With the way between us wide open, My blessings fall upon you in rich abundance. The greatest blessing is nearness to Me— abundant Joy and Peace in My Presence. Practice praising and thanking Me continually throughout this day."

—FROM *JESUS CALLING*, JULY 4

4. *What are some ways of building gratitude into your life throughout the day?*

_____

_____

_____

_____

5. *Why do you suppose gratitude is such an important way to God's heart?*

_____

_____

_____

_____

STUDY IT

Read aloud the following passage from John 12:1–8. This story takes place less than a week before Jesus' arrest and execution. Jesus knows the arrest is coming, but His disciples still don't want to believe it. Jesus and the disciples are having dinner with a family that has good reason for gratitude. Martha and Mary are the sisters of Lazarus, whom Jesus recently raised from the dead.

> Six days before the Passover, Jesus came to Bethany, where Lazarus lived, whom Jesus had raised from the dead. Here a dinner was given in Jesus' honor. Martha served, while Lazarus was among those reclining at the table with him. Then Mary took about a pint of pure nard, an expensive perfume; she poured it on Jesus' feet and wiped his feet with her hair. And the house was filled with the fragrance of the perfume.

But one of his disciples, Judas Iscariot, who was later to betray him, objected, "Why wasn't this perfume sold and the money given to the poor? It was worth a year's wages." He did not say this because he cared about the poor but because he was a thief; as keeper of the money bag, he used to help himself to what was put into it.

"Leave her alone," Jesus replied. "It was intended that she should save this perfume for the day of my burial. You will always have the poor among you, but you will not always have me."

6. *In Mary's culture women wore their long hair bound close to their heads, and it was considered shamefully provocative for a woman to unbind her hair in public. What did Mary do with her hair in this story? How would other people have interpreted this action?*

_____

_____

_____

_____

7. *Why do you think Mary did this? What was she communicating?*

_____

_____

_____

_____

8. *Think about how much money a year's wages represents today. What is the importance of giving our money to the poor? What is the importance of spending our resources on the worship of Jesus?*

_____

_____

_____

_____

_____

9. *How do you react to the idea of spending that much money on either of those things? What are typically your priorities with money?*

_____

_____

_____

_____

10. *What does passionate worship look like for you?*

_____

_____

_____

_____

11. *Read the passage aloud again. Take two minutes of silence to reread the passage, looking for a sentence, phrase, or even one word that stands out as something Jesus wants you to hear. Ask Him to help you hear Him. If you're meeting with a group, the leader will keep track of time. At the end of two minutes, you may share with the group the word or phrase that came to you in the silence.*

12. *Read the passage aloud again. Take two minutes of silence, asking Jesus what He is saying to you through the word or phrase you selected and whether He would like you to do anything in response. If you're meeting with a group, the leader will again keep track of time. At the end of two minutes, you may share with the group what came to you in the silence if you wish.*

13. *If you're meeting with a group, how can the members pray for you? If you're using this study on your own, what would you like to say to God right now?*

_____

_____

_____

LIVE IT

This week's daily Scripture readings include five psalms from a sequence called the Songs of Ascent. These "pilgrim psalms," sung by people journeying to Jerusalem for the annual festivals, expressed their desire for a life of passionate worship. Read each psalm slowly, pausing to think about what is being said. Rather than approaching this as an assignment to complete, think of it as an opportunity to meet with a Person. Use any of the questions that are helpful.

Day 1

Read Psalm 121. As majestic as the mountains are, the psalmist knows his help comes from Someone even more majestic. What reasons do we have for looking to the Lord alone for our help?

_____

_____

_____

How does it encourage you to know the Lord never sleeps?

In what circumstances do you need to know the Lord is watching over you? What is the main thing from this psalm you need to be sure of?

Thank the Lord for that thing and spend some time worshiping Him.

Day 2

Read Psalm 122. This psalm is about worshiping with others and going together to the house of the Lord. Why is that important?

What do you value about the house of the Lord where you worship with others?

Why does the psalmist value Jerusalem so much? How does he express his love for Jerusalem?

What is your Jerusalem? In what ways does your community need peace right now?

Pray for the peace of your worship community and thank the Lord for giving that community to you.

Day 3

Read Psalm 123. How do the eyes of a slave look to the hand of his master? How is that a good image for the way we should look to the Lord?

What mercy are you seeking from the Lord? What emotions are in your eyes as you look to Him for that?

What is bothering the psalmist that he expresses to the Lord in this psalm? What concerns do you want to express to Him with equal passion?

Tell God honestly what is going on in your life.

Day 4

Read Psalm 124. How does the psalmist's mood shift from the end of Psalm 123 to this psalm? What has changed for him?

_____

_____

_____

_____

How has the Lord been on your side? How does He show that even when you don't always get your way?

_____

_____

_____

_____

Why does the psalmist remind himself at the end that the Lord is the maker of heaven and earth? Why is that important to remember?

_____

_____

_____

_____

What flood threatens to engulf you? Or what flood has threatened you in the past that God has saved you from?

Praise God for the ways He has saved you from harm in the past and ask Him to keep saving you from harm now.

Day 5

Read Psalm 125. How are those who trust in the Lord like a mountain?

How is the Lord like the mountains around Jerusalem? Which of those images is most important to you today? Why?

In what area of your life do you need to trust in the Lord right now?

What does this psalm promise to those who live upright lives? What do you think living an upright life will involve for you today?

Ask the Lord to surround you with protection and empower you to live an upright life.

LEADER'S NOTES

Thank you for your willingness to lead a group through this *Jesus Calling* study. The rewards of leading are different from the rewards of participating, and we hope you find your own walk with Jesus deepened by this experience. In many ways, your group meeting will be structured like other Bible studies in which you've participated. You'll want to open in prayer, for example, and ask people to silence their phones. These leader's notes will focus on elements of the study that may be new to you.

CONSIDER IT

This first portion of the study functions as an icebreaker. It gets the group members thinking about the topic at hand by asking them to share things from their own experience. Some people may be tempted to tell a long story in response to one of these questions, but the goal is to keep the answers brief. Ideally, you want everyone in the group to have a chance to respond to the *Consider It* questions, so you may want to explain up front that everyone needs to limit his or her answer to one minute.

With the rest of the study, it is generally not a good idea to have everyone answer every question—a free-flowing discussion is more desirable. But with the *Consider It* questions, you can go around the circle. Encourage shy people to share, but don't force them. Tell the group they should feel free to pass if they prefer not to answer one of these questions.

EXPERIENCE IT

This is the group's chance to talk about excerpts from the *Jesus Calling* devotional. You will need to monitor this discussion closely so that you have enough time for the Bible study. If the group has a long and rich discussion on one of the devotional excerpts, you may choose to skip the other one and move on to the Bible study. Don't feel obliged to cover every question if the discussion is fruitful. On the other hand, do move on if the group starts to ramble or gets off on a tangent.

STUDY IT

Try to do the *Study It* exercise in session 1 on your own before the group meets the first time so you can coach people on what to expect. Note that this section may be a little different from Bible studies your group has done in the past. The group will talk about the Bible passage as usual, but then there will be several minutes of silence so individuals can pray about what God might want to say to them personally through the reading. It will be up to you to keep track of the time and call people back to the discussion when the time is up. (There are some good phone apps for timers that play a gentle chime or other pleasant sound instead of a disruptive noise.) If the group members aren't used to being silent in a group, brief them on what to expect.

Don't be afraid to let people sit in silence. Two minutes of silence may seem like a long time at first, but it will help to train group members to sit in silence with God when they are alone. They can sit where they are in the circle, or if you have space, you can let them go off alone to another room. As you introduce the exercise, tell them where they are free to go.

If your group meets in a home, ask the host before the meeting which rooms are available for use. Some people will be more comfortable in silence if they have a bit of space from others.

When the group gathers again after the time of silence, invite them to share what they experienced. There are several questions provided in this study guide that you can ask. Note that it's not necessary to cover every question if the group has a good discussion going. Again, it's also not necessary to go around the circle and make everyone share.

Don't be concerned if group members are quiet after the exercise and slow to share. People are often quiet when they are pulling together their ideas, and the exercise will have been a new experience for many of them. Just ask a question and let it hang in the air until someone shares. You can then say, "Thank you. What about others? What came to you when you sat with the passage?"

Some people may say they found it hard to quiet their minds enough to focus on the passage for several minutes. Tell them that's okay. They are practicing a skill, and sometimes skills take time to learn. If they learn to sit quietly with God's Word in a group, they will become much more comfortable sitting with the Word on their own. Remind them that spending time each day in God's Word is one of the most valuable things they can do for their spiritual lives.

PREPARATION

It's not necessary for group members to prepare anything for the study ahead of time. At the end of each study are suggestions for ways they can spend time in God's Word during the next five days of the week. These daily times are optional but valuable, so encourage the group to do them. Also invite them to bring their questions and insights back to the group at your next meeting, especially if they had a breakthrough moment or if they didn't understand something.

As the leader, there are a few things you should do to prepare for each meeting:

- *Read through the session*. This will help you to become familiar with the content and know how to structure the discussion times.

- *Spend five to ten minutes doing the Study It questions on your own.* When the group meets you'll be watching the clock, so you'll probably have a more fulfilling time with the passage if you do the exercise ahead of time. You can then reread the passage again when the group meets. This way, you'll be sure to have the passage even more deeply in your mind than group members do.

- *Pray for your group.* Pray especially that God will guide them to a deeper awareness of how to worship Him in all areas of life.

- *Bring extra supplies to your meeting.* Group members should bring their own pens for writing notes, but it is a good idea to have extras available for those who forget. You may also want to bring paper and additional Bibles for those who forget to bring their study guides.

Below you will find suggested answers for some of the study questions. Note that in many cases there is no one right answer. Answers will vary, especially when the group members are sharing their personal experiences.

Session 1: A Life of Rejoicing

1. *Answers will vary. The point of this question is to have the group members start telling each other their stories as they relate to the topic at hand: rejoicing. Those who had a solid foundation of rejoicing when they were young probably find it more natural to rejoice now, while those whose childhood homes did not cultivate joy in them may find it a new skill they need to learn. Those who had the advantage of a joyful home can take this opportunity to be grateful. Those who did not have that advantage can take this opportunity to be patient with themselves, knowing their past lack wasn't their fault. It's never too late to start learning joy.*

2. *Some of the reasons for rejoicing today include: God is present with us; He made this day; He has prepared abundant blessings in it; His glorious riches are more than adequate for our needs; His Peace is available.*

3. *Rejoicing will look different from person to person. Some personalities are quieter than others, so rejoicing for these individuals will mean a quiet smile and gentle attention to the good things around them. For others, rejoicing will be more vocal and demonstrative.*

4. *Some reasons to rejoice in our Love-relationship with Jesus include: it means we never need to feel lonely; we can know we are treasured beyond measure; we can recognize we serve a God who cares deeply for us and promises to always be with us.*

5. *Rejoicing in Jesus brings fulfillment now and in the future. He is real, now. Fantasy isn't real, so it can't bring genuine fulfillment. Fantasy also distracts us from doing the things in the real world God has given us to do—things that give our lives meaning.*

6. *Rejoicing in the Lord goes beyond just positive thinking or having an upbeat mood. It means rejoicing in our Love-relationship with Christ and recognizing all He has given us. It is rejoicing in who He is and what He has done for us. It is thinking about what we know about Him and taking joy in those things.*

7. *Paul advises us to pray for what we need and offer plenty of thanksgiving to God for what He has done and what He will do. Paul also advises setting our minds on uplifting things. This is more effective than worry because worry is the helpless attempt to control something that is out of our control, while prayer and thanksgiving connect us with the One who is in control and can be of real help in the situation.*

8. *Filling our minds with what is true, noble, right, pure, lovely, and admirable lifts our spirits, sets our thoughts on God's priorities, and creates healthy patterns in our thinking. While we shouldn't be in denial about the dark things in the world, to foster joy we need to avoid getting submerged in those things and seek godly alternatives.*

9. *So much of mass entertainment focuses on the dark, the violent, and the sexually twisted. If we have trouble sustaining joy, we should limit our diet of such things. There is enough darkness in real life.*

10. *Answers will vary. It's fine for this process to be unfamiliar at first. Again, be sure to keep track of time.*

11. *Answers will vary.*

12. *Answers will vary. Note that some people may find silence intimidating at first. Anxiety can move us to fill the air with noise, but taking a moment to be silent before God is good for us. Let the members express their discomfort, but let it be balanced by those who found the silence strengthening. Helping people become comfortable with silence will serve their private daily times with God in wonderful ways.*

13. *Take as much time as you can to pray for each other. You might have someone write down the prayer requests so you can keep track of answers to prayer.*

Session 2: A Life of Thankfulness

1. *Answers will vary. The goal here is for members to become aware of the degree to which thankfulness is or isn't a habit for them. If they have to work hard to come up with things they are thankful for, it could be their lives are especially difficult, but it could also be they are unaccustomed to noticing the blessings that surround them.*

2. *Thankfulness opens the door to God's Presence because it is an important part of any healthy intimate relationship. After all, our friends or spouses won't feel loved if we take their acts of kindness for granted and spew nothing but ingratitude and demands at them. God wants us to learn how to love, so He rewards us when we treat Him with love—and one of the main ways we treat Him with love is through thankfulness. Unlike our human relationships it is impossible to show love to God by giving Him things, because He doesn't need anything from us. However, He does desire our thankfulness.*

3. *Trust is the foundation on which thankfulness is built. If we are suspicious of God and mistrustful as to whether He is going to do anything for us, then we will be inclined to be ungrateful for the things He has already done for us. Mistrust makes us blind to God's past acts of goodness.*

4. *Some benefits of thankfulness include: it opens us to spiritual blessings; it helps us glimpse God's heavenly glory; it enables us to experience foretastes of heaven here and now, because it allows us to communicate intimately with God and receive communication from Him.*

5. *Thankfulness doesn't mean we ignore our problems or pretend they don't exist; rather, we simply balance our inborn tendency to pay attention to pain. Our brains are naturally wired to notice problems (pain) more than good things, because problems potentially threaten our survival. We don't have to work at noticing pain, but we do have to work at noticing and expressing thanks for the good things that God puts into our lives.*

6. *Answers will vary. The ingratitude of the nine is shocking in light of the great gift they were given. The gratitude of the one who returned is appropriate, but Jesus' original audience would have thought he was the least likely to be grateful because he was a Samaritan.*

7. *Jesus probably has in mind spiritual healing of the man as well as his physical healing. The man's faith expressed in gratitude opened him to healing from the disease of sin.*

8. *Answers will vary. An atheist would be one type of person whom we wouldn't expect to see rushing back to God.*

9. *Answers will vary. Make your group a safe place for people to be honest about this question, as they may never have thought about their level of thankfulness before. They may be embarrassed at how little they practice this habit when they really stop to consider it.*

10. *Answers will vary, but most of us need to make practicing thankfulness a deliberate act because of all the distractions we face each day. This could include putting reminders into our phone calendars, or posting Scripture verses where we will see them each day, or doing something else to prompt us to pause and thank God. Incorporating thanksgiving time into your group's prayer time is another good way of building this practice.*

11. *Answers will vary.*

12. *Answers will vary.*

13. *Responses will vary.*

Session 3: A Life of Confession and Forgiveness

1. *Answers will vary. The group members don't need to feel embarrassed about where they fall on this scale, because it is largely a matter of inborn temperament and childhood upbringing. It's not better to be a 1 or a 5 on this scale. Those who tend to be blind to their faults may need feedback from other people in order to grow in holiness. Those who are quick to blame themselves may be distracted from growth when they fault themselves for things that aren't sins. Either way, it's helpful to know our natural bent so we can get the most out of a habit of confessing our sins, which is the topic of this session.*

2. *God already knows all about our sins, so we don't need to be ashamed of revealing something He didn't know. Also, His children are clothed in Jesus' righteousness, so God isn't going to respond to our confession with wrath. In fact, He is eager to help us stand when we've fallen. He has the power to help us avoid the same sin in the future.*

3. *An example of self-pity would be feeling sorry for ourselves for being lonely and unloved when in fact our weak or broken relationships are partly the result of our sins against other people—sins we are hiding from and therefore can't stop committing.*

4. *Guilt is painful, and we often seek to numb its pain through some pleasurable sin such as gossip, complaining, gluttony, or sexual sin. Guilt also saps our energy, so we have less enthusiasm for continuing on the path Jesus has for us.*

5. *Answers will vary. There may be one or two people in your group who are having trouble walking in the freedom of forgiveness, so be sure your group is a safe place for them to say so. If no one wants to talk openly about the sins that are weighing on them, you can offer to talk privately after the meeting with anyone who is having trouble believing God has forgiven them for something.*

6. *God was letting the psalmist feel the weight of guilt in order to motivate him to repentance and confession.*

7. *Some of the blessings of forgiveness include: we feel less burdened with guilt; we choose a better path rather than being sucked by habit into the same sin again and again; the lines of communication with God are open, so we can pray freely and be confident our prayers are heard; we are more able to sense God's Presence. All of these things make life better for us.*

8. *Many people avoid confessing their sins because it requires humility, and they have too much pride to admit they're at fault. In addition, confession requires placing ourselves under God's authority—another thing that runs counter to pride. Shame, which is from the enemy, also hinders godly confession.*

9. *Each of us at one time or another has likely felt our sins are too bad for God to forgive. But John insists they are never beyond forgiveness because God is greater, and He is faithful (trustworthy) and just (He always does what accords with justice, and Jesus has satisfied the penalty for every believer's sin).*

10. *The benefit of stopping right at the moment of sin is that it forces us to immediately recognize where we have gone wrong. However, this only works if we actually notice what we're doing and take time to address the issue. The advantage of setting aside a few minutes at the beginning or end of the day for confession is that we give focused attention to our actions. The benefits of being accountable to a trusted friend is that he or she may be able to see potential dangers in our lives more clearly than we can see them ourselves. A good friend can point out these potential sin patterns, pray with us and for us, and help guide us through the situation.*

11. *Answers will vary.*

12. *Answers will vary.*

13. *Responses will vary.*

Session 4: A Life Free from Idols

1. *Answers will vary. Possibilities include money, success, control, our children's success, a romantic relationship, possessions, what other people think of us, maintaining our routine, physical health.*

2. *Most of us fear change at one time or another. If we avoid it and cling to routine, or if we get upset at others when they suggest change, we probably fear it.*

3. *Answers will vary and may overlap with the answers people gave in question 1. Routine is one possible example of what makes us feel secure; other possibilities include money, work, a particular person's love, children doing well, success, being in charge, other people's approval, or open opportunities to choose. It's hard to recognize our idols, so this is another way of getting at the matter.*

4. *Signs we are treating status as a god include: focusing all our efforts on keeping up appearances; trying to always "keep up with the Joneses"; spending too much time or resources on things that make us look better to others; having an unreasonable desire to please other people. Signs we are treating another person as a god include: deferring to what he or she wants or says even if it conflicts with the Bible's teaching or damages our emotional or spiritual health; feeling our lives would be over if we lost that person; fearing that individual's disapproval more than we fear God's; putting his or her "wants" ahead of other people's needs.*

5. *It is both safe and wise for us to let go of false gods because they never satisfy; rather, they stir up our desires to have more and more—and those desires can lead to downfall. But God does satisfy. When we seek Him, we experience His Joy and Peace.*

6. *God has rescued His children from slavery to sin and its consequence: death. We're not always as gripped by the value of that gift as we need to be, because other needs feel so demanding.*

7. *God is jealous in the sense of wanting to be number one in our lives. This is for our protection. He is unwilling to share us with other "lovers"; they only want to use us. He is holy and true—there is no one else like Him. He made us; He saved us from sin and death; He provides for all of our needs. All these things make Him deserving of first place in our affections.*

8. *Someone or something will always take first place in our lives. That someone could be ourselves or another person, or it could be an intangible like success or material possessions. It's impossible to have two top priorities, so it's impossible to have both God and things be foremost in our lives. Also, a god is a master. If we have more than one voice telling us what we must do, we will be torn in two. It's impossible to obey two conflicting voices.*

9. *Money is an attractive god because it buys what we need to survive physically: food, clothing, shelter. It also buys comfort, other people's respect, entertainment, and a host of other desirable things.*

10. *We should rely on God rather than wealth because God is the ultimate source of everything we need for our existence—not just physically, but also spiritually and emotionally. He is permanent, everlasting, and utterly reliable. Even more, He is the source of eternal life.*

11. *Answers will vary.*

12. *Answers will vary.*

13. *Responses will vary.*

Session 5: A Life of Seeking God's Thoughts

1. *Answers will vary. Note that none of these natural preferences is better than another—this is just a chance for your group members to become aware of how they're made and to get to know each other better. This question will also prepare members for the first of the readings that follow, which is about how to handle a tendency to make plans and cling to them. For members who prefer to be spontaneous, overplanning won't even be a temptation.*

2. *The reading doesn't say planning is bad or useless; in fact, it can be extremely valuable. What the reading does do is challenge those of us who cling too tightly to our plans. Spontaneous people aren't necessarily more dependent on God's guidance than planners are; they just express their self-dependence differently. Spontaneous people still make decisions about what they are going to do, and those decisions need to be open to correction by God's agenda. Whichever type of person we are, we need to submit our intentions to God and give Him the freedom to override our preferences.*

3. *The main item in searching for God's way is to persistently check in with Him throughout the day. When we get to the end of a task and look at our to-do list, it's time to say, "What next, Lord? Do you have something different for me?" Also, when someone makes a request of us, we need to pause, pray, and wait for an answer about it before we say yes or no.*

4. *Thankfulness takes the sting out of adversity by giving us the joy of experiencing God's Presence in the midst of it. It also opens us to God's thoughts—we can see God's perspective on our circumstances. You might ask a follow-up question: "Has anyone in the group experienced thankfulness taking the sting out of adversity?" If so, they can share their experience. We discussed thankfulness in session 2, so this is a good chance to check in and see if anyone has increased their practice of thankfulness and how that has affected them.*

5. *Thankfulness can help us to see our circumstances from God's point of view. We may get a glimpse of what He is accomplishing through our situation. Ingratitude keeps our minds stuck in a narrow track in which it's hard to see alternative ways of responding to a situation. Thankfulness helps us notice God's goodness, His wisdom, and His power. It helps us see there is a bigger picture than the narrow view of our fears.*

6. *Some of the ways we seek the Lord include: communicating with Him through prayer; hearing Him and understanding Him through His Word; pleasing Him through loving our neighbor; being willing to be guided by Him; asking the Holy Spirit to empower us.*

7. *God's thoughts are higher than our own because He sees everything—how our lives fit into His overall plan, and how they interact with the lives of others. God also sees the truth of where we are and how we got there (we typically have blind spots about this), and He knows where our choices will take us. He has full knowledge of the wisest decision in any situation and is always urging us to choose the most loving action, whereas we often look for the safest route or the one that suits our desires.*

8. *This is a good question for everyone to try to answer. Note that their example of what getting their way looks like doesn't need to involve a huge issue—it can be as simple as how they want tomorrow's work day to go.*

9. *Answers will vary. God's way might be seeking the good of the other people involved in the situation, or it might involve training in perseverance, courage, or humility. Regardless, it is always God's will for us to love our neighbors as we love ourselves (see Matthew 22:39) and seek others' interests ahead of our own (see Philippians 2:3–4).*

10. *Isaiah 55:6–11 promises God's desires and purposes will always—* **always**—*be accomplished. Not even our sin can ultimately thwart God's purposes. His desire is for us to seek Him, forsake any evil ways or unrighteous thoughts we have, and rely on His mercy. When we do, God promises He will "freely pardon" us.*

11. *Answers will vary.*

12. *Answers will vary.*

13. *Responses will vary.*

Session 6: A Life Close to God

1. *Answers will vary. The major distractions may at first seem to be the tasks we are expected to do—such as work and childcare—or distractions like the Internet and social media. But in reality, our real distractions are more likely to be the monologue in our heads: worries, desires, resentments, fantasies. If nobody names these, you can mention them and ask if anybody can identify with those distractions. Note that it's not necessary to go into detail about the content of people's worries or desires.*

2. *Answers will vary, but living close to God involves having a personal relationship with Him. When we develop a pattern of staying close to God, we find ourselves turning to Him first when a problem or need arises instead of trying to figure out everything on our own or relying on other human beings. As we stay near Him, He guides our steps and leads us down the paths that He wants us to take.*

3. *Answers will vary, but they likely include any negative habits or patterns of thinking that keep us so wrapped up in our own worries, desires, resentments, and fantasies that we don't have mental space for attending to God.*

4. *Answers will vary.*

5. *If our worries, desires, resentments, and fantasies are crowding God out of our minds, then a first step toward living closer to God would be to offer those distracting thoughts to God. Make them the subject of prayer. We can pray, "Jesus, this is what dominates my thoughts today. Please enter into that space and fill me with Your thoughts." We can set an hourly reminder sound on a phone to remind us to pause and check in with God about what has been dominating our thoughts. In this way we will build a habit of gently turning our minds to God.*

6. *The Father prunes us by allowing suffering into our lives. Sometimes that suffering is just some small way in which we don't get what we want in a given situation. We have to contend with a limitation and choose perseverance and humility (or their opposites, quitting and proud bitterness). Sometimes the suffering is something large. Either way, the Father does this not because He enjoys seeing us in pain but because the character qualities that grow in adversity enable us to bear fruit for Him. Certain character traits will **only** blossom through pruning.*

7. *To remain or abide in Jesus is to maintain conscious contact with Him throughout the day. We do this in many ways, such as by praying throughout the day, by asking to be filled with the Holy Spirit, and by maintaining connections with other Christians. We also do it by obeying the things Jesus has told us to do, such as making God's kingdom our top concern (see Matthew 6:33), and loving others as He loves us (see John 15:10–13).*

8. *We must remain in Jesus because we can do nothing of value apart from Him. This is startling but true. We can do lots of self-interested things apart from Jesus, but love requires connection to Him—and love is what matters. Also, a terrible fate awaits those who don't remain in Jesus: "such branches are picked up, thrown into the fire and burned" (John 15:6). This is a reference to hell. Remaining in Jesus isn't an optional part of the Christian life. It's central.*

9. *Obeying Jesus is one of the main ways we stay connected to Him. This can trouble us if we are aware of how far short our behavior falls from His standard of love. But if we are genuinely committed to growing in love, He is eager to empower us. We simply need to ask for insight and power, open our eyes to others' needs, and step out in faith. Jesus' commands are not burdensome (see 1 John 5:3) but enliven us.*

10. *Answers will vary. Without naming names, you can share a time when you needed God's power to love someone.*

11. *Answers will vary.*

12. *Answers will vary.*

13. *Responses will vary.*

Session 7: A Life of the Beauty of Holiness

1. *Answers will vary. The point of this question is to help members think about what the word **beauty** conjures up for them. The word is much debased and abused today, so we need to peel back some of its connotations to get at the glory and splendor the psalmist had in mind when he used the word in the Bible passage you're going to study.*

2. *God does many things to create loveliness in us, but this reading concentrates on **one** thing: He clears out negative things in our souls, making room for His Spirit to take full possession. We need to be willing to let go of anything He chooses to take away. An example might be a selfish habit of being wrapped up in our own concerns that keeps us from noticing others' needs.*

3. *Answers will vary. Almost any circumstance might qualify: a situation at work, a health challenge, a problem with a son or daughter.*

4. *Answers will vary. If your group members live in an urban environment or have weather that makes getting outdoors difficult at this time of year, they may have had little contact with the natural world recently. But enjoying nature is extremely good for the soul because it points us to our Creator. Talk about ways we can bring nature into our homes: growing plants and really looking at them from time to time, or finding a tree (even a bare one) and studying its bark. These are things God made that reflect His order and beauty.*

5. *We tend to have a narrow notion of what makes a face beautiful: youth and symmetry. Talk about the beauty of aging faces and bodies, of eyes, of smiles, of strong hands.*

6. *What sets God apart from idols is the fact He is alive and He made the world. He alone has the power to make a universe, the wisdom to understand it, and the goodness to care for it. Everything else we might worship—money, power, status—has no life in and of itself. These are things that God has made, and they are all less than He is.*

7. *The psalmist here is talking about the majesty of the temple in Jerusalem. The fact that God commanded a beautiful worship space be built for Him indicates He is worthy of the very best. While authentic worship can happen in sparse or unattractive surroundings, beauty affects us. The character and ambience of a building communicates to us even if we're not aware of it, just as the beauty of nature can lift our thoughts to all that is glorious about God. Some people are less sensitive to beauty and more concerned with practicality, so those in your group may represent an alternate point of view. Still, there is beauty even in order and function.*

8. *Answers will vary. Some feel the psalmist wants us to worship God for His beauty—His holiness is beautiful. Others think the passage is inviting us to adorn ourselves with holiness—holiness in us is beautiful, and God is interested in transforming us so we have loveliness of character. Others think of incorporating beauty into our worship through music, architecture, and other arts, as well as by bringing the beauty of nature into our worship of God.*

9. *The trees, heavens, and sea worship the Lord by fulfilling their places in the natural order God has created. For example, trees don't try to be what they're not or take over the planet—they have their place, and they worship God by flourishing in that place. The stars worship God by doing what He made them to do rather than rebelling. They are naturally beautiful, and their beauty glorifies their Maker.*

10. *Awe is an emotion of mixed fear, reverence, and wonder. It's an emotion we feel in the presence of something much greater than ourselves or something exceptionally grand and magnificent. We feel awe in the Lord's presence because He is infinitely greater than us in power, wisdom, and sheer vastness. Everything that exists would cease to be if it weren't for the Lord sustaining its existence. We feel awe when we contemplate the size and power of our sun, and the sun is a tiny speck in the universe God has made. We should feel small, weak, and dependent when we contemplate the Lord's magnificence.*

11. *Answers will vary.*

12. *Answers will vary.*

13. *Responses will vary.*

Session 8: A Life of Tender Passion

1. *Answers for this final icebreaker question will vary. Use this first question as a way for the members to reflect on the most important principle they took away from the study.*

2. *We were created to glorify and enjoy God. It's the reason why we exist, so it should be a higher priority than anything we do to make ourselves feel comfortable. A structured life is at best a means that helps life go more smoothly. It's a good thing, but it's not the most important thing. If glorifying God brings some messiness into our lives, takes away some of our feeling of control, that's okay.*

3. *Structure can help believers create routines that develop their relationship with God, such as regular times for prayer, Bible study, and fellowship with other Christians. However, too much structure can lead to a desire for control, which can cause us to rely on our own strength instead of turning to God for support. There is no reason for those who are more naturally inclined toward structure to feel bad about being made this way—they simply need to be alert to those times when their natural tendencies conflict with glorifying the Lord through worship and serving others.*

4. *There are many ways we can build gratitude into our lives, such as by using an hourly calendar reminder or building a habit of expressing thanks for every meal. We can then expand that practice to express thanks at moments when our minds have free space, such as when we're driving or standing in line at the grocery store. We could even make a game of looking for things to be grateful for and share the game with a buddy, texting messages of gratitude back and forth.*

5. *Gratitude is glue in any relationship, so it shouldn't surprise us it is glue in binding us to God and God to us. God doesn't need anything from us, but He wants relationship. He has done (and is doing) so much for us, and His joy blooms in us as we notice it and thank Him for it.*

6. *Mary not only unbound her hair in public but also used it to wipe Jesus' feet. This was an incredibly intimate act that would have seemed sensual, even erotic. But everyone at the dinner knew Mary and knew Jesus, so they would have known her intention wasn't carnal. They would have seen her using her hair, regarded as a woman's most glorious attribute, to wipe Jesus' feet, considered a person's most lowly body part. This was a dramatic gesture of humiliation. With the perfume added to the gesture, it was clearly an act of self-abasing worship.*

7. *Jesus had restored Mary's brother, Lazarus, to life through an astounding miracle, demonstrating to her that He was the Son of God. She knew He would soon be arrested and likely killed. In fact, she seems to have understood these things far more clearly than Jesus' disciples did. By anointing Him with perfumed oil (typically a part of ancient burial rites), she honored Him in the face of approaching death. She abased herself to express gratitude and worship.*

8. *God cares deeply about the poor, and He wants the care of the poor to be a priority for us (see Deuteronomy 15:7–11; Galatians 2:10; James 1:27; 1 John 3:16–18). Yet this story in John's Gospel suggests that spending money on the worship of Jesus is also important. Ask the group to think of some ways in which we do this today—such as by investing time to serve in our church, or by spending money on a worship album that helps focus our thoughts on Christ, or by taking a friend out to coffee to bless that person. The twin great commandments are to love God with all our being and to love our neighbor (see Matthew 22:27–40). Our generous use of money expresses our love to God and love for our neighbors.*

9. *Answers will vary. We tend to spend our money on our own needs and desires and those of our families. This makes generosity to God and our neighbor difficult for us. We rightly recognize what Mary did was rare and astonishing, yet the story is in the Scriptures partly to encourage us to do likewise.*

10. *Answers will vary. Some people are vocal and demonstrative by nature, while others are quieter. Notice that Mary didn't say anything; she simply did something profoundly symbolic. Passionate worship may involve any number of offerings—lifting our voice in praise, or a generous gift of money or time, willing service to God and others, or extended time in prayer.*

11. *Answers will vary.*

12. *Answers will vary.*

13. *Responses will vary.*

ENJOY JESUS' PRESENCE.
FIND COMFORT
IN HIS PEACE.